SEARCH THE SCRIPTURES 2

SEARCH THE SCRIPTURES 2

Topical Questions and Answers

Modupe O. Adeleye

To order additional copies of this book, contact:
Xlibris Corporation
1-888-795-4274
www.Xlibris.com
Orders@Xlibris.com
98704

CONTENTS

DEDICATION

This book is dedicated to
God the Father,
God the Son
and
God the Holy Spirit.
It is also dedicated to all
Born Again Christians of the World.

ACKNOWLEDGEMENT

This is to acknowledge God the Father, God the Son, and God the Holy Spirit for the continuous insight and the enablement which brought about this book—"Search the Scriptures 2"

I also acknowledge all heads of Churches and leaders of different Denominations that had contributed to the completion of this book.

God's anointing on you will daily increase more and more.

I also appreciate the participation of my family members in the accomplishment of this work.

I thank everybody that was involved in making this work a success.

God bless you all and grant you your hearts' desires.

FOREWORD

This Book "Search the Scriptures (2)" as the name connotes, will make you "search the scriptures" for in depth knowledge, about the word of God.

Jesus Christ our Saviour, was aware of this when He commanded His disciples to search the scriptures, because the scriptures testified about Him. (John 5:39)

Believers should follow the example of the early Christians who found solace in searching the scriptures so that they might not go astray from the commandments and statues of God.

Joshua 1:8 says "This book of the law shall not depart out of thy mouth but thou shall meditate therein day and night that thou mayest observe to do according to all that is written therein, for then thou shall make thy ways prosperous and then thou shall have good success". You can discover avenues to prosperity and success from searching the scriptures.

Psalm 119:11 says "Thy word have I hid in mine heart that I might not sin against thee". If all Christians will search the scriptures and through it know what is right to be done at all times, they will not sin against God.

Psalm 119:105 says "Thy word is a lamp unto my feet and a light unto my path". Without the word of God, people will be groping in darkness.

We christians are enjoined to know the word of God in its fullness so that we may be led by it and not go astray from the path of our Maker.

This book is therefore recommended to all Christians for a daily right walk with God, and to counteract the arrows and wiles of our enemy.

Professor I.O.A. Adeleye
Bowen University
(of the Nigerian Baptist Convention)
Iwo, Osun State, Nigeria.

INTRODUCTION

This book contains lots of questions on topics from the Bible.

The topics dealt with in this Book range from day to day matters to Bible based events.

The questions are also accompanied by Bible references to make the answers more explicit in line with the first Book.

This book is educative, relaxing entertaining and an eye opener.

Above all, it makes the user an expert in the word of God and in the events recorded in the Bible.

This Book will also be very useful as easy Bible reference.

Christians need to store much of the scriptures in their memories so that they may be battle axes for God.

Be blessed as you use this book.

QUESTIONS

(1)   ## THE HORSES

Match the kings listed on the left, to the events at the right.

1.	Pharaoh	a.	He honored a man by letting him ride the royal steed through city streets
2.	Ahab	b.	He crippled captured chariot horses, except for 100, which he kept for his own use.
3.	Hezekiah	c.	He lost all his horse-drawn chariots in a sea
4.	Solomon	d.	When his army panicked and fled, he rode a horse to escape the enemy
5.	Amaziah	e.	During a famine, he set out with another man to find grass to feed his horses and mules
6.	Jehu	f.	This richest and wisest of kings had 4,000 stalls for horses and chariots
7.	David	g.	The king of Assyria promised him 2,000 horses if he had that number of soldiers left from a battle who could ride them
8.	Jehoshaphat	h.	This fast charioteer rode to Jezreel to find king Joram
9.	Ben-hadad	i.	Killed by assassins in Lachish, he was carried to his grave on horseback
10.	Ahasuerus	J.	He agreed to go to battle with king Jehoram telling him "my horses are thy horses"

(2)   ANGER

1. Which king became so angry with his son that he hurled a spear at him?
2. Which king was angry because the man he asked to curse his enemies blessed them three times instead?
3. When God abandoned his plan to destroy Nineveh which prophet became angry?
4. Who, when he saw the Israelites worshiping a calf idol, ground the graven image into powder and sprinkled the dust on water for them to drink?
5. Which soldier became angry with his young shepherd brother because he left his sheep to come and watch a battle?
6. Which prime minister became so angry when a man refused to bow to him, that he planned to destroy all Jews throughout the kingdom?
7. When a man refused to sell a vineyard, which king became so angry that he went to bed without eating?
8. Who afflicted with leprosy, became angry with a prophet's suggestion for his healing?
9. Which king was angry because his nightmare could not be interpreted and ordered the execution of all the wise men in Babylon?
10. Who became angry because his father-in-law pursued him and searched his belongings
11. Who became so angry with his people that he struck a rock instead of speaking to it?
12. Who incurred the anger of God because of disobedience of not destroying all the enemies and animals?

(3)   ANOINTING

Match the left names with the anointing on the right

1.	Elijah	a.	After the priest anointed this new king with oil from the tabernacle, a trumpet blew and the people rejoiced.
2.	Aaron	b.	He was anointed by having a vial of oil poured on his head by Samuel.
3.	Jesus	c.	He had orders to anoint a plowman
4.	Jehu	d.	Following instructions from God, he looked over eight young men then finally took the horn of oil and anointed the last one he had viewed.
5.	Jacob	e.	After being clothed with special garment he and his sons were anointed
6.	Joash	f.	He was anointed king over Israel by a young prophet who ran outdoors after the anointing
7.	Saul	g.	A woman anointed this man's feet with ointment
8.	Daniel	h.	After this seven-year old boy was anointed king a wicked queen was killed.
9.	Samuel	I	He anointed a stone that he had used as a pillow
10.	Solomon	J	During a mourning period of three weeks, he fasted and refrained from anointing himself

(4)   ARK OF GOD

The following list contains 11 events concerning the ark, but they are not in sequence. Determine which event happened first and list the others according to how they happened.

Ark is brought to Jerusalem

Ark was placed in Solomon's temple

Ark was brought to Obed-edom's house

John saw the ark in God's temple in heaven

Philistines took the ark

Ark was carried in the march around the walls of Jericho

Uzzah touched the ark and was killed

Ark remained at kirath-jearim for 20 years

Ark was to be made according to God's instructions

Philistines returned the ark

Ark was used to divide the river Jordan

(5)   BATHING /WASHING

1. Who found a baby at the river?
2. Who washed his face after an emotional meeting with his young brother?
3. Which governor washed his hands before a crowd to prevent a riot?
4. What two men stopped and washed their hands and feet in a basin at the entrance to the tabernacle whenever they neared the altar?
5. Who invited angels to wash their feet and spend the night at his house?
6. Who before starting a journey to Bethel with his family had them destroy idols, bathe and put on fresh clothing?
7. Who gave a travelling servant and the men accompanying him water to wash their feet?
8. Which king while walking on his palace roof saw a beautiful woman bathing?
9. Who mentioned taking a bath in snow?
10. Who instructed a blind man to go and wash in the pool at Siloam which resulted in the man regaining his sight?

(6)　　　　COURAGEOUS PEOPLE

Match the names of these courageous people with their brave deeds.

1.　Daniel

a. Accompanied by only an armor bearer he climbed into an enemy garrison and killed some 20 men.

2.　Aaron

b. He dared to attack vast armies of Midianities and Amalekites with only 300 men.

3.　Shammah

c. He killed two lion-like men and a lion in a pit of snow.

4.　Joseph of Arimathea

d. During a terrible plague in which thousands of people died, he bravely mingled with the stricken people to make atonement for them to God.

5.　David

e. Aware that going before a king without his summons meant death this person disobeyed the decree in an effort to save the Jews.

6.　Gideon

f. He disregarded a king's edict against petitioning God and continued praying even though it meant being thrown to lions.

7.　Esther

g. Even though his life was threatened by Sanballat and Tobiah he refused to hide in a temple behind bolted doors.

8.　Beneaiah

h. After Jesus crucifixion he dared to ask Pilate for Jesus body

9.　Nehemiah

i. When deserted by his soldiers, he stood alone and struck down enemy Philistines.

10.　Jonathan

J. He dared to face an enemy giant, armed with only a sling and stones for a weapon.

(7)   BUSINESS

Match the persons at the left with his or her business dealings at the right.

1.	Esau	a.	He used unfair labour practices in his brick-making establishment.
2.	Ornan	b.	This person sold purple cloth
3.	Lydia	c.	He set up a widow in the oil business.
4.	Nehemiah	d.	He sold his threshing floor
5.	Hanamel	e.	He sold his birthright to his brother.
6.	Paul	f.	He sold to a widower a burial ground.
7.	Ephron	g.	While a prisoner, he sold a field to his cousin.
8.	Elisha	h.	He sold his brother to a camel caravan.
9.	Pharaoh	i.	He was in the tent-making business with a man-and-wife team.
10.	Judah	j.	He banned the Sunday sale of goods in Jerusalem.

(8)   CHARIOTS

1. In battle, who took 1,000 chariots from King Hadadezer and "houghed at the chariot horses"?
2. Which prophet had a vision of four chariots, each drawn by a different colored horse, coming from between what looked like two brass mountains?
3. Who was made "to ride in the second chariot" of King Pharaoh?
4. Whose war chariots were lost in the Red Sea?
5. Who had "cities for chariots" for his 1,400 chariots?
6. Who had 900 iron chariots, and made life unbearable for the Israelites for 20 years?
7. When "there appeared a chariot of fire and horses of fire", who watched his friend depart heavenward in the vehicle?
8. Who had the reputation of driving "furiously"?

9. Which King, wounded in battle, died in his chariot and was brought to Samaria where "one washed the chariot in the pool of Samaria"?
10. Who brought a magnificent chariot and horses and hired 50 footmen to run ahead?

(9)   CITIES

The events listed at left happened in the cities listed at right. Match them together.

1. This city's walls fell on 27,000 men	a. Nob
2. When this city was threatened by an enemy, King Hezekiah shut off its waterworks.	b. Samaria
3. Pharaoh gave this burnt city to his daughter for a gift	c. Kirjath-sepher
4. By capturing this city, a man was given Caleb's daughter for a wife	d. Ephesus
5. This city was destroyed by fire and brimstone	e. Jericho
6. Eighty-five priests were slain in this city	f. Shechem
7. At the sound of trumpets and men shouting, this city's walls fell flat	g. Jerusalem
8. This besieged city suffered such terrible famine, a woman boiled and ate her son.	h. Gezer
9. Books worth thousands of dollars were burned at a public bonfire in this city.	i.Sodom
10. This city was beaten down and sowed with salt.	j. Aphek

(10)   **CONFESSIONS**

Select the appropriate name from the following list to answer each question.

Aaron   Achan   Balaam   Daniel   Ezra   Woman with issue of blood

John   Moses   Pharaoh   Saul   Shimei

1.   Who, after beating his mule, confessed to an angel that he had sinned?
2.   Who, after stealing battle spoils, confessed to his theft and was stoned to death?
3.   Which captive, wearing sackcloth and ashes, confessed his sins and the sins of Israel to God?
4.   Who wept, as he lay on the ground in front of the temple making a confession, and was surrounded by a great crowd of men, women and children?
5.   Who was instructed to lay both hands on the head of a life goat and confess the sins of the Israelites?
6.   Who was confronted by priests and Levites when he confessed, "I am not the Christ"?
7.   Who had people being bitten by poisonous snakes come to him, to confess their sins and ask him to pray for the removal of the snakes?
8.   Which king, after confessing to a prophet, took hold on him and tore his robe?
9.   As King David was crossing the river Jordan, who confessed his regret for throwing stones at David?
10. After a hailstorm, who confessed to Moses and Aaron that he and his people were wicked?
11. Who confessed touching the helm of a healer's garment and was healed.

(11)   HIDING

Match the correct names with the events.

Adam	David	Elijah	Jesus
Joash	Joshua	Moses	Obadiah
Rahab	Saul		

1.   Who, when he heard five kings were hiding in a cave, had great stones rolled against its mouth and guards posted?
2.   Who hid in a field to escape a jealous king who wanted to kill him?
3.   Which little boy was hidden in God's house for six years to save him from being murdered?
4.   Who was told by God to hide by Cherith Brook and eat the food supplied by ravens?
5.   Who "took a hundred prophets and hid them by 50 in a cave and fed them bread and water"?
6.   Who hid two spies among flax stalk on a roof.
7.   Who hid from God among garden trees?
8.   Which baby was hidden by his mother for three months to save him from being killed by Pharaoh?
9.   Who hid from antagonistic Jews who "took up stones to cast at him"?
10. Who had "hid himself among the stuff" and had his hiding place revealed by God?

(12)   JESUS

Match the events to where they happened.

a. Jerusalem	e. Capernaum	
b. Emmaus	f. Bethany	i. Gadarenes
c. Nazareth	g. Cana	j. Jordan
d. Galilee	h. Gethsemane	

1.   Where Jesus raised Lazarus from the dead
2.   Where Jesus turned water into wine
3.   Where the Holy Ghost, as a dove, descended on Jesus

4. Where Jesus caused demons to go out of a man and into a herd of pigs.
5. Where Jesus rode a colt and people strewed branches along His path
6. Where Jesus went into a synagogue and was given the book of the prophet Esaias
7. Where Jesus was betrayed and arrested
8. Where Jesus appeared to the 11 disciples
9. Where Jesus taught in the synagogue
10. The resurrected Jesus walked along with two of his followers to this village

(13)   COVENANTS

Match one of the names with each of these events

Abraham	Jehoiada	Moses
Benhadad	Jonathan	Nahash
Isaac	Joshua	Noah
Jacob	Jesus	

1. Who, after making covenant with his father-in-law, set up a pile of stones as a witness to their act?
2. Who, after making a covenant with a dear friend, gave him his robe, armor, sword, bow and girdle?
3. Who, after a rainstorm, was told by God that the sight of a rainbow in the clouds would be a covenant between Him and every living creature?
4. Who, after making a covenant with the people at Shechem, set up a great stone under an oak as a witness?
5. After making a covenant with a king who had once hated him, who made a feast for the royal party?
6. Who, after God made a covenant with him, had his name changed?
7. Who agreed to make a covenant with the men of Jabesh if he could gouge out the right eye of every citizen?
8. Which king sat in Ahab's chariot and made a covenant with him, promising to restore cities his father had taken?
9. Who stood between God and the Israelites at Horeb on the occasion when God made a covenant with them?

10. Which priest "made a covenant between the Lord and the king and the people" followed by the people breaking down all the altars of Baal?
11. He was the Testator of the New covenant"

(14)   DEATH/MIRACLES

1. Which queen met her death by being thrown from a window and trampled by horses?
2. Which prophet performed mouth-to-mouth resuscitation on a dead boy and restored him to life?
3. After having his skull broken by a thrown mill-stone, who had his armor bearer kill him so that "men say not of me a woman slew me"?
4. Which dressmaker was restored to life by Peter's prayers?
5. Which king when he was wounded in battle died in his chariot?
6. Who died on a mountaintop after being stripped of his garments?
7. Which man having been dead for four days, was restored to life?
8. Who fell down dead after he had lied about a property deal?
9. Who met his death on the gallows he had built for another man?
10. Who committed suicide by hanging because his advice was not taken?

(15)   DECEPTION

1. Using goat skins, who helped a son to deceive his father?
2. Who deceived an escaping captain telling him he would be safe in her tent, then, after giving him a drink of milk murdered him?
3. Afraid of recognition by king Achish who deceived him pretending "himself mad in their hands and scrabbled on the doors of the gate and let his spittle fall down upon his beard"?
4. By wearing old clothes carrying mouldy provisions and pretending to be ambassadors whom did the Gibeonites try to deceive?
5. On his wedding night, who was deceived by his father-in-law
6. Which king angered a witch because he had tried to deceive her by disguising himself?
7. Which two men at different times deceived kings by telling them their wives were their sisters?

8.   By deceiving a king's attendants, telling them he had a message for their king, who got to see the fat king alone and stabbed him to death?

9.   Who deceived his brothers by pretending not to know them, then accused them of being spies and threw them into jail?

10. Who sent a woman of Tekoah disguised as a mourner to deceive David?

(16)   SWORDS

Match the names at the left with the events at the right.

1. Eleazer   a. This defeated man had his head cut off with his own sword

2. Saul   b. About to attack a formidable opponent, he refused to use a sword, saying, "I have not proved it"

3. Joshua   c. He fought Philistines until his hand became too tired to hold his sword

4. Abimelech   d. To settle an argument between two women he threatened to cut baby in halves with a sword.

5. Peter   e. During a battle, he and his son were the only ones equipped with sword

6. Abner   f. At the point of death caused by a woman he said to the armor bearer, "Draw thy sword and slay me, "that men say not to me, a woman slew him" And his young man thrust him through.

7. David   g. He "lifted up his eyes and looked and behold, there stood a man over against him with his sword drawn in his hand"

8. Joab   h. As he and another general sat on opposite sides of the pool of Gibeon, he watched while there was mortal sword play between their young men.

9. Solomon   i. With his sword he slashed off the ear of a servant.

10.   Goliath   j.   While pretending to greet a man with a kiss, he stabled him with a sword

(17)   DREAMS/VISIONS

The persons at left saw in a dream, or vision, the events listed at right. See if you can match them.

1.   Joseph   a.   The Lord sitting upon a throne surrounded by seraphims who cried, "Holy, holy, holy is the Lord of hosts"

2.   Zechariah   b.   A barley cake tumbled into an army camp and overturned a tent.

3.   Nebuchadnezzar   c.   The sky opened up, letting down a great canvas sheet filled with a variety of animals, snakes and birds.

4.   Isaiah   d.   A tree that kept growing higher and higher into the sky until it could be seen by everyone in the world.

5.   Jacob   e.   "A man riding upon a red horse, and he stood among the myrtle trees . . . and behind him were red horses speckled and white.

6.   Daniel   f.   Seven fat cows coming out of a river

7.   Soldier   g.   A beast with great iron teeth; "it devoured and broke in pieces, and stamped the residue with feet of it"

8.   Peter   h.   While pursuing a man, he had a dream in which God told him not to bless or curse the man.

9.   Pharaoh   i.   Angels going up and down a ladder that reached to heaven.

10. Laban   j.   "The sun and the moon and the 11 stars made obeisance" to him.

11. Stephen   k.   He saw the heavens opened and the son of men standing on the right hand of God.

(18)   ESCAPES

Match the persons with the escapes

1.	Paul	a.	He escaped on horseback from enemy Israelites
2.	Abiathar	b.	After this murderer escaped to Seirah, he blew a trumpet and mustered an army.
3.	Jacob	c.	When he heard wicked cities were going to be destroyed he escaped to Zoar.
4.	Elijah	d.	With the help of his wife, who let him down of a window, he escaped from his father-in-law, who was trying to kill him.
5.	Lot	e.	Being warned by an angel in a dream, he escaped to Egypt with his wife and child.
6.	Joseph	f.	To escape stoning by the Jews, he "escaped out of their hand" and went beyond Jordan.
7.	Benhadad	g.	To escape his brother, who wanted to kill him, he fled to his uncle.
8.	David	h.	While Doeg was carrying out a wholesale slaughter of priests, he was the only one who managed to escape.
9.	Ehud	i.	To escape a vengeful queen, he "arose and went for his life and came to Beersheba.
10.	Jesus	j.	Disciples let him down a wall in a basket so he could escape enemy Jews.

(19)   ALTAR MATTERS

1. Who, following God's instructions, built an altar and laid his son on it as a burnt sacrifice?
2. Who, while waiting for two friends in Athens, saw an altar inscribed "To the unknown God"?
3. Who was given the nickname of Jerubbaal after he knocked down the altar of Baal?
4. Which King, while visiting Damascus, saw an unusual altar and had Urijah, the priest, build one just like it in his hometown?

5. Who built an altar out of stones on Mount Ebal and carved each of the Ten commandments on the stones?
6. Which King, because he disobeyed God's command and burned incense on a holy altar, was stricken with leprosy?
7. Which general of David's army murdered two generals, and was slain at a tabernacle altar as punishment?
8. Which angry king's arm became paralyzed after he threatened the prophet who said an altar would split apart with its ashes spilled to the ground?
9. Who, after building an altar at Beersheba, had his servants dig a well?
10. Which king had bones taken from mountainside graves, and burned them on an altar at Bethel to defile it?

(20)   SPY

1. Who sent men to spy out Canaan, telling them to bring back fruit on their return?
2. Who hid two men sent to spy on Jericho, on a roof, covering them with flax stalks?
3. Which king believed servants sent by David to his land were spies, and "shaved off the one half of their beards and cut their garments in the middle?
4. Who had tricky questions put to him by spies that they might take hold of his word" and "deliver him unto the power of the governor"?
5. Which governor accused his brothers of being spies to see "the nakedness of the land"?
6. Which spy was rewarded with a piece of land?
7. Who had his house invaded by five spies who confiscated his idols and images and had six hundred men with weapons at the gate?
8. Which missionary was spied upon by "false brethren" as they waited for a chance to arrest him?
9. Who sent spies throughout "all the tribes of Israel", instructing them that when they heard a trumpet sound they should announce him as king?
10. Which fugitive in the wilderness sent spies to locate his pursuer, a king?

(21)   **FAMILY AFFAIRS**

Answer the questions below from the following list:

Abimelech	Jacob	Paul's nephew
Abraham	Jethro	Virgin Mary
Hagar	Jezebel	Sennacherib
Jehoshabeath	Jonathan	Job's wife
Jesse	Lois	
Jesus	Miriam	

1. Which woman hid her little nephew from her vengeful grandmother in a storage room in a temple?
2. Who had 70 of his brothers killed on one stone?
3. Which grandmother was commended by Paul for her great faith?
4. Which man gave good advice to his son-in-law, who was wearing himself out counseling people?
5. Who, banished to the wilderness, put her child under a bush to die?
6. Which girl watched to see what would happen to her baby brother who was in a floating cradle?
7. Who became angry with his father, left the table, and refused to eat all day?
8. Who armed his servants and rescued his nephew who had been taken prisoner by enemy kings?
9. Which father had to parade his eight sons before a prophet?
10. Who encouraged her husband, the king to do every sort of evil?
11. Who advised her husband to curse God?
12. Whose nephew saved him from enemies plot?
13. Which cousin went to visit another cousin in pregnancy?
14. Who placed his mother and brothers in second position to his divine mission?
15. Who was helped by the daughter of his mother's brother?
16. His sons smote him and killed him as he worshiped in the house of his god?.

(22) FARM MATTERS

Select the appropriate name to match the event.

Boaz	Job
Gibeon	Joseph
Isaac	Naboth
Jesus	Samson
Joab	Uzziah

1. Which farmer winnowed his barley at night?
2. On a Sabbath, who, with his companions, went through cornfields and picked ears of corn to eat?
3. Who beat out wheat in a winepress to hide it from the Midianites?
4. Which king, besides having a host of fighting men, "had also much cattle . . . husbandmen also, and vine dressers in the mountains . . . for he loved husbandry"?
5. Who had his barley crop set on fire because he refused to meet with Absalom?
6. Who was told by a messenger that "the oxen were ploughing and the asses feeding beside them, and the Sabeans fell upon them and took them away"?
7. Who reaped a tremendous crop, one hundred times the grain he sowed?
8. Who, during a famine, gave food and seed in exchange for Egyptians' cattle and land?
9. Who turned 300 foxes with burning tails loose into a grain field?
10. Who refused to give his vineyard to a king because it was "the inheritance of my fathers" and was killed?

(23)   FASTING

Match each person at the left who fasted, to the description of his or her fast, listed on the right.

1.	David	a.	He fasted in sorrow for several days after hearing of the destruction in Jerusalem
2.	Paul	b.	When he finished fasting, a man appeared before him clothed in a bright robe.
3.	Jesus	c.	He fasted 40 days and nights while on a mountain top with God.
4.	Ahab	d.	He fasted for three days after losing his sight
5.	Esther	e.	After being fed by an angel he fasted 40 days and nights.
6.	Moses	f.	After having a man cast into a lion's den he spent the night fasting.
7.	Nehemiah	g.	He fasted and lay all night on the ground when his child became ill.
8.	Cornelius	h.	After fasting 40 days and nights he was tempted to change stones into bread
9.	Darius	i.	Fasted for three days and nights before making a forbidden appearance before a king.
10.	Elijah	j.	After being reproached by a prophet, he tore his clothes, put on sackcloth and fasted.

(24)   FEAR

1. Which man was so frightened by a dream his hair stood on end?
2. Who was "greatly afraid and distressed" when he was about to have a reunion with a brother he had wronged, and learned his brother had 400 men with him?
3. Which king, at the sight of a vast army of enemy Philistines, was "afraid and his heart greatly trembled"?
4. When he saw an angel ascended in an altar's flame, who fell face down to the ground in fear?

5. At the sight of handwriting on a wall, who became so frightened his knees knocked together?
6. Who, as a passenger on a ship, was tossed overboard when sailors became frightened during a "mighty tempest in the sea"?
7. Who were frightened of a man who came down from a mountain with a shining face?
8. Who tried to walk on water, but was terrified at the sign of high waves and began to sink?
9. What band of fugitives "were sore afraid" at the sight of 600 Egyptian chariots coming in pursuit of them?
10. Which three men "were sore afraid, when a voice came out of a bright cloud, and said, "This is my beloved son, in whom I am well pleased"?

(25) CELEBRATIONS

1. When handwriting appeared on a wall, who was holding a feast for a thousand guests?
2. Which man had seven sons who always celebrated their birthdays with a feast?
3. Which man, after he "held a feast in his house like the feast of a king", became drunk, and the next morning suffered a stroke?
4. Who gave a feast to celebrate his son's weaning?
5. Which king held a seven-day feast in the palace garden while his queen feasted with the women inside the palace?
6. Who, while entertaining 30 young men with a feast that lasted seven days, challenged them with a riddle?
7. Which king on his birthday gave a feast for all his servants?
8. Which publican entertained Jesus with a great feast at which many other publicans were present?
9. Which man, after giving a progress report to King David, was entertained, along with his 20 companions, with a feast?
10. At the dedication of the temple, who held a feast that lasted 14 days?
11. Who was the wayward son that had a feast held for him at his return home?

(26)   GATES

**Each person on the left had an encounter with a gate. These events are
described on the right. See if you can match them.**

1.   Absalom

   a.   So happy at hearing Peter's voice at a gate,
        the servant ran inside an left him standing
        outside.

2.   Peter

   b.   He stabbed Abner to death at Hebron's gate
        to avenge a brother's death.

3.   Elisha

   c.   When a priest heard this man prophesying,
        he put him in stocks that were located in a
        high gate by the temple.

4.   Rhoda

   d.   He sat at the gate and spoke to his kinsmen
        concerning the purchase of a land with the
        foreign widow of another kinsman

5.   David

   e.   He escaped from a besieged city by way of
        palace garden gate.

6.   Ezra

   f.   He went to the city gate early every morning
        to hold a kangaroo court session in trying to
        win people from his father.

7.   Samson

   g.   He took the doors of the gate of a city and
        the two posts and went away with them.

8.   Zedekiah

   h.   Standing before Jerusalem's Water Gate,
        he read the book of the Law to a crowd of
        people.

9.   Joab

   i.   This king stood by a city gate and reviewed
        an army that marched past him by the
        hundreds and thousands.

10. Boaz

   j.   While escaping from jail, this prisoner
        saw the gate to the street open by its own
        accord

11. Jeremiah

   k.   He prophesied that at the gate of Samaria a
        measure of flour and two measures of barley
        would each be sold for a shekel

(27)   GIFTS

1. Who, before meeting with an estranged brother, sent to him a gift of many cattle, his thought being, "I will appease him with the present that goeth before me . . . peradventure he will accept me"?
2. Which sick king, after receiving a gift sent by the king of Babylon, showed all his treasures to the messengers who brought the gift?
3. Who, because he interpreted a king's dream, was "given many great gifts"?
4. After watering a traveling servant's camels, who was given an earring and two bracelets?
5. Which sick king sent 40 camel loads of gifts to a prophet with the question, "shall I recover of this disease"?
6. Who told his servant that they had no gift to offer the man of God "called seer" when they wanted to make inquiries from him.
7. Which man, when his lost fortunes were restored by God, was given a piece of money and a gold earring by each of his friends?
8. Which newborn baby was given gifts by men who had traveled a long way to find him?
9. Which man was given a gift of 20 cities "and they pleased him not"?
10. Who, after testing a king with questions, gave him gifts of gold, spices and precious stones?

(28)   JEALOUSY

1. When he heard women praising a man's battle victory with song, who became jealous?
2. When God accepted this brother's firstborn sheep as an offering, who became so jealous and turned into a murderer?
3. Who was the personal assistant of Moses that became jealous of Eldad and Medad when they prophesized?
4. Who was arrested because the Jewish leaders were jealous of his popularity with the people?
5. Who made Philistines so jealous, because of his success with cattle and crops, that they filled up his wells with earth?
6. Name Jesus' parable in which a brother became jealous because his father celebrated another son's return form his wasteful spending with a feast.

7. Which jealous woman was responsible for having a slave girl and her son banished to the wilderness?
8. Who was sold into slavery because his jealous brothers believed their father "loved him more than all his brethren"?
9. Which two preachers were expelled from a city because of jealous Jewish leaders?
10. Which childless woman was jealous of her sister's fertility?

(29)   HAIR

1. Which mother promised God if He gave her a baby boy no razor would ever touch his head?
2. In a vision, who was suspended between heaven and earth by a lock of hair?
3. Who cut his hair only once a year, and the cut hair weighed about three pounds and was too heavy to carry around?
4. Who had a vision in the night that was so frightening it made his hair stand up on end?
5. Who, in a letter, said that Christian women should be noticed for being kind and good, and not by the way they dress—or make their hair.
6. Who lost his incredible strength when he was given a haircut?
7. Who, after he had cursed children who had mocked his hairless head, had the horrible experience of seeing 42 of them killed by two bears that came out of the woods?
8. Which king, after being banished from his palace, had his hair grow as long as eagles' feathers?
9. Who told the multitude before him that even the hairs of their heads were numbered in the sight of God?
10. Which hairy man had his father's blessing taken away by a conniving mother?

(30)   HEAVEN

Each of the following actions was experienced by different people. Name the people.

1.   Which leader, being harassed by hungry people, was told by God, "Behold, I will rain bread from heaven and the people shall go out and gather a certain rate every day"?
2.   Who dreamed of a tree "Which reached unto heaven"?
3.   Who was told to "look now towards heaven and tell the number of the stars"?
4.   After he finished a prayer, who saw fire come down from heaven and consumed his offering and sacrifice in the house of the lord?
5.   Who had a vision of heaven "opening, and a sheet, knit at the four corners, let down to earth"?
6.   Who, after being baptized, had the heavens opened to him and saw the Spirit of God coming down in the form of a dove?
7.   Which man's prayer caused the sun to stand still "in the midst of heaven" so that the Israelites might "avenge themselves upon their enemies?
8.   Who was carried by a whirlwind up to heaven?
9.   Which prophet was standing by the river at Chebar with captives when he saw the heavens open and a vision of God appear?
10. Who saw an angel standing between earth and heaven with a drawn sword stretched out over Jerusalem?
11. Who decided to build a tower up to heaven?
12. Who saw the heaven open and the son of man standing at the right hand of God?

(31)   EARTHQUAKES

1.   Who, in company of the Israelites, met with God and the "Whole mount quaked greatly"?
2.   During whose attack on a garrison, "the earth quaked: so it was a very great trembling"?
3.   Which prophet invoked an earthquake while he was standing on a mountaintop?

4. Who had a vision of an earthquake that leveled a tenth part of a city, killing 7,000?

5. Who, at his death, "the veil of the temple was rent in twain from the top to the bottom; and the earth did quake, and the rocks rent"?

6. Which two men, while prisoners, felt a great earthquake shake the prison foundations and had their cell door opened?

7. Which three men, who rebelled against Moses, were punished by having the earth "clave asunder" and the "earth opened her mouth and swallowed them up"?

8. Name the two women who were looking at a sepulcher when an earthquake occurred, and an angel descended from heaven and rolled back the stone from the door.

9. Who, when God delivered him from enemies, composed a song that described an earthquake: "Then the earth shook and trembled; the foundations of heaven moved and shook"?

10. In the days of which king did people flee from an earthquake?

(32) ELIJAH OR ELISHA?

Elijah and Elisha both performed miracles, and actions sometimes similar ones and some others different. Who performed the following?

1. Poisonous pottage made edible
2. River Jordan divided
3. A sack of corn and 20 loaves of barley fed 100 men
4. Life of a child restored
5. Caused fire to fall and consume an altar with its sacrifice, and evaporate water in a ditch
6. A man's leprosy healed
7. Oil supply multiplied
8. The waters of Jericho purified with salt
9. Caused an ax head to "swim in water"
10. Called down fire that destroyed army captains and their men.
11. Handed over to a king some captured armed men
12. Caused 42 children to be eaten by bears
13. He anointed an administrator as king of Israel
14. His time experienced lack of rain for three years
15. Made a dishonest servant leprous

16. He left his oxen to take up God's work
17. Dead man raised in his tomb
18. Helped a barren woman to give birth.
19. Transported to heaven in a chariot of fire

(33) MARTYRS

Match these martyrs with their sufferings

John the Baptist	John	Philip
Peter	Mathias	Mark
Andrew	Simon (Zelotes)	Stephen
Thomas	James the less	James the great
Mathew	Jude	Bathlomew

1. He translated the Gospel of Mathew into India language. He was Martyred in America
2. He was dragged to pieces by the people of Alexandria at the great solemnity of serapis their idol.
3. At the age of 94, he was beaten, stoned and finally had his brain dashed out with a fuller's club by the Jews.
4. He labored in North Asia. He suffered martyrdom at Heliopolis in Phrygia. There, he was scourged thrown into prison and afterwards crucified in AD 54.
5. He was cast into a cauldron of boiling oil but escaped miraculously without injury. He was later banished to the Isle of Patmos where he wrote a book in AD. 96. He was the only apostle who escaped a violent death.
6. He preached to many Asian Nations. He was crucified on a transverse cross at Edessa
7. He preached the Gospel in Mauritania, Africa and in Britain. He was crucified in A.D.74
8. He labored in Parthia and Ethiopia. He was slammed with a halberd into the city of Nadabah A.D. 60.
9. He felt unworthy to be crucified like Jesus. He therefore asked to be crucified upside down during the reign of Nero.
10. He was hanged on an olive tree by the idolatrous priest of Greece.
11. He was cast out of the city and stoned to death.(Acts 7).

12. He was beheaded by Herod through the request of Herodias, Phillip's wife (Mark 6,14-29).
13. He was elected to fill the vacant place of Judas. He was stoned in Jerusalem and was then beheaded.
14. He was led out of the city and beheaded during the reign of Nero.
15. He was beheaded by Herod in Jerusalem (Acts 12).
16. He preached the Gospel in Parthia and India. He was thrust through with a spear and killed.
17. He was commonly called Thaddeus. He was crucified at Edessa A.D 72.

(34)   ANGELS

At left hand are 12 people who had dealings with angels. On the right are the locations of their meetings. Match them.

1.	Jesus	a.	As she sat in the field
2.	Gideon	b.	House
3.	Peter	c.	City gate
4.	Abraham	d.	Oak tree
5.	Shepherds	e.	Sepulchre
6.	Ornan	f.	Juniper tree
7.	Hagar	g.	Threshing floor
8.	Elijah	h.	Field
9.	Cornelius	i.	Prison
10.	Lot	j.	Wilderness spring
11.	Mary	K	Tent door
12.	Manoah & wife	l	On mount of Olives

(35)   KINGS

1. Which king with his wife deceived a prophet when the wife went to the prophet to know whether their sick child would live?.
2. Which king's mother was Naamah?
3. Which king's seventy sons were killed?
4. Which king called a great prophet, "father"?

5. Which king was described as doing what was not right in the sight of the Lord like David his father but walked in the way of the kings of Israel?

6. Which king trusted in the Lord for his help against the threat of his enemies?

7. Which king started to reign in Jerusalem at the age of twelve, reigned fifty five years and his mother's name was Hephzibah?

8. Which king's hand got withered when he was insulting a man of God sent to warn his people against evil doings?

9. Which king ordered that James the son of Zebedee be killed and after wards imprisoned Peter.

10. Which king was the first husband of Herodias who was taken by his brother who killed John the Baptist?

11. Which king began with prophesying and ended up with witchcraft?

12. Which king overstepped his boundary by using the vessels taken from the Temple at Jerusalem to entertain his (1000) guests?

13. Which king sold himself to work wickedness in the sight of the Lord and was encouraged by his wife?

(36) GOD'S MESSENGERS

Match the list on the left to the persons who took the actions:

1.	He was sent to save the Jews from their task masters.	a.	Ahasuerus
2.	He was sent to deliver a message of what would happen to his master's family to him	b.	Jesus
3.	She was sent to deliver her people from destruction	c.	Mordecai
4.	He was sent to deliver the Jews from national adversity	d.	Esther
5.	He was sent to make a niece a Queen.	e.	John the Baptist
6.	It was a king that announced his greatness. Who was the person?	f.	Samuel

7. He was sent to prepare the   g.   Peter
    way of the Lord.
8. He was sent to deliver an unbeliever h.   Moses
    from his evil path.
9. He was sent to deliver all   i.   Joseph
    sinners from hell fire.
10. Who was sent to deliver and   j.   Joshua
    divide the promised land to the Israelites.

(37)   GOD'S INTERVENTION

Match the left and right phrases to make complete actions.

1 The Red sea which brought   a. Were the ones taken
   deliverance to the Israelites   captive instead

2 The pillar of fire which gave   b. Killed those who threw
   light to the Israelites   them into the furnace

3 The night which brought   c. Brought total
   deliverance and joy to the   termination to his
   children of Israel   enemies

4 The den of lions that moved   d. Was eventually used to
   Daniel to promotion   cut off his own head

5 The fairy furnace which   e. Brought lamentation and
   became an air-conditioner to   tragedy to Egypt.
   the Hebrew children

6 The sword which Goliath   f. Shall go back to the
   meant to cut off the head of   wicked
   David

7 The Syrian soldiers who came   g. Gave darkness to the Egyptians.
   to take Elisha in Dothan

8 The stones and arrows that   h. Brought destruction to
   the wicked may fire at the   the Egyptians.
   righteous

9 The gallows Haman made for   i. Became his own burial
   Mordecai   ground

(38)   THOSE WHOSE NAMES WERE CHANGED

The following people had their names changed.
Which new names were they given and by whom? The following are their original names.

1.   Jacob
2.   Oshea
3.   Simon
4.   Saul
5.   Daniel
6.   Hananiah
7.   Mishael
8.   Azariah
9.   Benoni
10.   Abram
11.   Sarai
12.   Hadassah

(39)   BIBLE COMMON NAMES

1.   How many people do you know in the Bible that bear JUDAS? Find them out?
2.   Locate this name in the Bible. ELIEZER.
3.   How many people are called MARY in the Bible?
4.   Locate all where TAMAR was mentioned in the Bible
5.   Locate those who were called SIMON in the Bible
6.   Locate JOSEPH in the Bible
7.   Search for JOEL
8.   Search for DEBORAH
9.   SIMEON, locate this name in the Bible.
10.   JAMES—How many do you know?
11.   JONATHAN—Bring out all where the name is mentioned.
12.   JOSHUA—who had this name in the Bible
13.   JUDAH locate this name
14.   Search for GAIUS
15.   ELIHU—How many can you see in the Bible?

(40) INJURIES

Can you give the names of those who are involved in these injuries?

1. Who was the king that fell down through a lattice in his upper chamber and was injured?
2. Who had the hollow of his thigh touched and it got dislocated during a wrestling with an angel?
3. Whose foot was crushed against a wall by an ass?
4. Which king was fatally injured when a woman threw a milestone down on him?
5. Give the name of the king who passed the judgment of dividing a baby between two mothers?
6. Which five year old boy became lame when he fell from the hand of a maid?
7. Whose ten children were killed when a building fell on them?
8. Give the name of the person who was hung on a tree by his long hair?
9. Who fell backward and broke his neck being an old and heavy man?
10. He was bitten by a snake as he laid sticks on a fire. Who was he?

(41) SIGNS AND WONDERS

1. On whom did God multiply His signs and wonders?
2. Who saw the signs and wonders of God?
3. Who gave the Israelites the advice not to follow anybody who would show signs and wonders to lure them from God?
4. What would be upon the Israelites as signs and wonders if they refused to keep God's commandments?
5. Who are for signs and wonders referred to in Is. 8:16?.
6. Who again in the New Testament gave the advice that believers should not follow false christs and false prophets that might want to show them signs and wonders?
7. Whom did Jesus say would not believe it they did not see signs and wonders?
8. Who performed signs and wonders that brought fear upon every soul in the time of Pentecost?.

9. Who performed signs and wonders among the Gentiles?
10. According to Job, who does great things that cannot be fathomed and wonders that cannot be numbered? (NIV).

(42)   CONSPIRACIES

1. Which kings conspired against Ahaz, the son of Jotham the king of Judah?
2. Who conspired against his father causing him to flee from Jerusalem with his entire household?
3. Which chariot captian conspired against his king and killed him when the king was drunk?
4. Whose brothers were jealous of him and conspired to sell him?
5. Which priest was slain by Saul because Saul thought he conspired with David against him?
6. On which apostle did forty Jews had a conspiracy and vowed not to eat until they had killed him?
7. Which man did his wife conspire with his enemies to destroy the source of his strength so that they might capture him?
8. Which king was compired against by his servants who murdered him in his house at Millo?
9. Who was the successful administrator whose other colleagues conspired against him and had him thrown into the lions' den?
10. Which two men led a conspiracy to prevent the wall of Jerusalem from being built?
11. Who was betrayed when one of his followers in exchange for money conspired with Jewish leaders to kill him.
12. Which husband and his wife conspired to tell lies to a group of Jesus followers?
13. Which mother conspired with a son to deceive her husband?
14. Which king and wife conspired to deceive a man of God?

(43)   MOTHERS

1. Who was the mother that stole her own father's idol?
2. Who was the mother who gave his son a bad name because of the events that happened when she was giving birth to him?
3. Which mother lost her two sons when her family went to live with in another tribe?
4. Give the name of the mother who taught her son the scriptures and faith in God.
5. Which mother wept at a prayer convention when she was asking God for a son?
6. Mention the name of the mother who asked for envaiable positions for her sons?
7. What was the name of the mother who left his under age son in the Temple when they went to worship?
8. Who was the mother of a preacher always dressed in clothes made with camel's hair and linen girdle?
9. Whose mother taught him a prophecy of what he should do and not do as a king?
10. What was the name of the mother of the king of Israel who did what was evil in the sight of the Lord as his father did?
11. Which mother was removed from being queen because she had made an idol in the grove?
12. Which mother gave her son advice concerning an interpretation of the words written on the wall during a party?
13. Which mother hid her son in an ark of bulrushes?
14. Who was the mother of the additional six sons of Abraham?
15. Who was the mother of the most precious son among the patriarchs?
16. Which mother was not loved by her husband and yet gave birth to 6 sons and a daughter for the husband?
17. Which mother cast his son under a shrub to die when their bottle of water finished.
18. Who was the mother of Jezreel, Loruhamah and Loammi?
19. Which mother did his son bring his wife to her tent to live immediately the wife was brought to him?
20. What was the name of the mother of Amasa who was the sister of David?.
21. Which mother took a sharp stone and circumcised his son?.

(44)   FATHERS

Answer these questions below:

1.   Which father had eight sons and the last was given recognition?
2.   Whose son conspired against him?
3.   Which father wanted to kill his own son because he supported a rival candidate for his throne?
4.   Who was the father of sons that sinned against God by laying with the women that assembled at the door of the tabernacle in Israel under their father?
5.   Who was the father of the man to whom David restored Saul's possession?
6.   Give the name of the father who sent a servant to his own tribe and kindred to get a wife for his son?.
7.   Which father was deceived by his son with the help of his mother?
8.   Who was the father that took dowries for his two daughters from the same man?
9.   To which father did an angel appear to instruct him and his wife on how they should bring up the special child to be born by them
10. Which father had twelve sons and a daughter?
11. Which father was dumb until the day of the naming of his son?
12. Whose two sons married the same woman but she never had a child for any of them?
13. Which father gave his daughter to a husband that he did not know?
14. Who was the father of Queen Esther and the uncle of Mordecai?

(45)   SERVANTS

1.   Who was the servant who received an outstanding power when his master was elevated into the sky?
2.   Which servant tried to force a grieving woman away from a sympathetic prophet?
3.   Which servant told his master of an impending destruction over his family?
4.   Who was the servant that led his master's grandson to a new king, who was eager to help him to reap the good deeds of his father.

5. Which servant would have inherited his master's heritage if the master had been childless?

6. Which servant ran away from his master but was later reconcided to him as a brother of the same faith?

7. Who was the servant that later became the mother of the master's first son.

8. Who was the servant who gave birth to the seventh and eight sons of the children of the head of the family?

9. Which servant gave birth to Dan?

10. Whose servant was made to swear by the Lord when the master wanted to send him to accomplish an important mission?

11. Who was the servant of God that was made to sin after serving God meritoriously?

12. Who was the servant that was thrown into prison because of false accusation?

(46)   ACTIONS

Match the left persons with the actions performed by them.

1.	Woman with the issue of blood	a	He climbed a tree
2.	Naaman	b	He leaped over a wall
3.	Samson	c	He out ran another runner by taking a short cut across a plain
4.	Jacob	d	He dipped in a river seven times
5.	Miriam	e	He walked on water
6.	Ahimaaz	f	He caused rain to fall after a drought
7.	Zacchaeus	g	He drove furiously
8.	David	h	He carried the door of a city gate to the top of a hill.
9.	Elijah	i	She took a timbrel in her hand and danced
10.	Peter	j	He wrestled with an angel until the breaking of the day
11.	Jehu	k	She touched the helm of His garment

(47) BUILDINGS

1. Which wall builder, when threatened by an enemy had his men build with a tool in one hand and weapon in the other?
2. Which brick makers faced a problem when their straw material was taken from them and they were ordered to continue to turn out the same quota of bricks?
3. Who led the building of the Lord's temple without the sound of hammer or an ax?
4. Who received building plans from God and was ordered to construct a sizeable boat?
5. Which clever craftsman was specifically appointed by God to serve as general superintendent of the construction of the tabernacle?
6. Which king built cities on mountains and castles and towers in forests?
7. Which clever worker was brought to Jerusalem for the purpose of making artistic brass items for the temple.
8. Which king was forbidden from building a temple for God because his hands were stained with blood.
9. Who put a curse on anyone who would rebuild a city that was destroyed by the Israelites on their way from Egypt to Canaanland.
10. Who built the first city and named it after his son?
11. Which city, and tower did the disobedient descendants of Noah build as a monument of human pride and so that they would not be scattered over all the earth?

(48) PRAISES AND SONGS

Match the persons at the left to the praises and songs listed at the right.

1.	John	a.	At the end of a meal they sang a hymn, and then went to a mountain
2.	Josiah	b.	While in a dungeon with another man, he sang hymns at mid night
3.	Jehoshaphat	c.	He had a vision of a choir 144,000 strong, singing a new song before God's throne, but "no man could learn that song but the 144,000 which were redeemed from the earth"

4. Moses

   d. At the death of two men, he composed a dirge for them and commanded that it be sung throughout Israel

5. Saul

   e. This slain king was mourned by temple choirs, and to this day sad songs are still sung about the death

6. Barak

   f. At the end of this man's life, God gave him a song he was to teach to the children of Israel

7. Silas

   g. He had a choir lead the march into battle, and when they began to sing, the Lord "set ambushments" against the enemy

8. Israelites

   h. After winning a battle with the help of a woman, he sang with her a song of victory

9. David

   i. He became jealous when singing women included another man in their songs of praise

10. Disciples

   j. When a well was dug, they sang a song

11. Who sang a song with the women after the Lord had defeated their enemies?

12. They only sang songs of praise and blew trumpet and a city wall fell.

13. She sang a song when the Lord gave her a son

14. She sang a song when she went to visit her cousin who was also pregnant.

15. He sang a song at the naming of his son

16. He sang a song with baby Jesus in his hand

17. They sang a song for their miraculous release from the prison.

18. He praised God who redeemed his life and brought him back to his throne.

(49)   HOSPITALITY

1. He implored the angelic visitors to wash their feet and refresh themselves under a tree.
2. Who suggested that their family should make a chamber for a man of God with a bed, a table, a stool and a candle stick?
3. Who offered to prepare a kid for an angel that advised him to offer it to the Lord?
4. Who brought in two angels from the gate of the city and lodged them over night only to be troubled by his towns men?
5. Who was "the son of Abraham" who received salvation because he received his "Guest" willingly and joyfully?
6. Who after baptism besought the disciples to abide in her house?
7. Who entertained a king in making with his servant in the chiefest place among others?
8. Who was a "stranger in a strange land" that was entertained for helping some ladies to water their flocks?
9. Who was entertained when a lot of republicans were also invited?
10. Who entertained a servant sent on an errand to look for a wife for his master's son?

(50)   LETTERS

1. He wrote a letter that was to lead to the death of the messenger who delivered it?
2. Who sent a letter of plot to kill an innocent man because of his possession?
3. Who wrote a letter to a king who had not walked in the way of his father or in the way of the king of Judah?
4. Who sent a letter of command for the healing of his general?
5. Who sent out a letter of invitation for Passover to be held in Jerusalem
6. Who wrote a letter of threat to another king to downgrade his God?
7. Who wrote a letter to stop the work of the temple building.
8. Who wrote a letter of instructions to the Gentiles?
9. Who sent a letter for the destruction of a king's seventy sons?
10. Who sent a letter to save an apostle from the plot of those who wanted to kill him?

(51)   DRUNKENNESS

1. Who was drunken and became naked in his tent?
2. Whose wife saw him drunken and delayed an important talk with him till the following morning?
3. Who after he and his guests were drunken, saw the fingers of a man's hand wrote on the wall?
4. Whose daughters caused him to be drunk and thereby became the father of their children?
5. Whose servant with half of his chariots conspired against him when he was drunk?
6. Which church did Paul instruct to make sure that during Lord's Supper some should not be drunken while some have nothing to drink and eat.
7. Which king was busy drinking and got drunk even at war time which led to his defeat.

(52)   DISOBEDIENCE

1. The disobedience of this couple led to the fall of man.
2. The disobedience of this man led to a disgraceful defeat of the Israelites on their way to the Promised Land.
3. Who was it that had no regard for God and disobey His instruction that he should let His people go?
4. Who disobeyed God's instruction to go and preach in a town but went his own way?
5. Which king because of greed disobeyed God and was therefore rejected by God?
6. Which prophet did God send to Bethel but obeyed man rather than obeying God's instructions?
7. Whose disobedience prevented him from getting to the promised land?

(53)   MURDER

1.   Who committed the first murder?
2.   Who slew his 70 brothers to become a king?
3.   Who killed another warrior because he wanted to avenge his brother's blood?
4.   Which king ordered the killing of a man because of the king's lust of the flesh and lust of the eye.
5.   Who plotted a killing so as to take possession of the murdered person vineyard
6.   Who murdered Zachariah king of Israel during the thirty and eighth year of Azariah king of Judah?
7.   Which king of Judah did that which was evil in the sight of the Lord served and worshipped idols and his servants murdered him?
8.   Who was killed for denouncing a marital misconduct of a ruling family?
9.   Who was murdered by his two sons when he was worshipping in the house of his god?

(54)   FAITHFULNESS

1.   Who was faithful to a point of giving up his son?
2.   Who was so faithful that his accusers could not find an occassion of fault in him?
3.   Who because of his faithfulness did not count his life precious to him?
4.   Who was the servant that was absolutely faithful to his master?
5.   This man received punishment for his faithfulness
6.   The master of this man was bold to say that he was faithful
7.   Even a prophet was not afraid in the face of death to declare that this man was faithful. Who is the man?
8.   He was a friend in deed

(55)   PRAYERS

1. Who were the people who sang and prayed in the prison?
2. Who prayed that his destiny be changed?
3. Who prayed that God should not put the Israelites to shame when they were defeated by a small nation?
4. Who prayed that God should be merciful to a sinful town if a few righteous people were found there?
5. Who prayed from the overwhelming sorrow of her heart in the temple?
6. Who commanded fire down through his prayer?
7. He prayed that God should heal him and save him from destruction
8. Who prayed by confessing his own sins and the sins of his nation?
9. Who prayed for forgiveness of disobedience from the fleshy prison he found himself?
10. Who prayed to raise up a dead lady?
11. She was a widow of eighty years who served in God's presence
12. He prayed to bring a dear friend back to life
13. Which king prayed and stirred up God's vengeance against the confederation of his enemies.

(56)   PROPHETS

1. Who was a senior brother that was made a prophet to his junior brother?
2. Who was the prophet that was employed to curse the people of God?
3. Which prophet single handedly faced four hundred and fifty man strong opposition?
4. Which prophet knew the secrets of the enemies even at the planning stage?
5. Who was the prophet who saw the vision of four living creatures and had their appearance described vividly?
6. Which prophetess ruled in Israel and made a conquest over the enemies?
7. Which prophet had an harlot as a wife?
8. Though, this man was not a prophet by descent, but God used him as a prophet for Israel.

9.   Who was the prophet that brought the shadow ten degrees backward by his cry to the Lord?
10. Which Prophet did God send to rebuke a King?

(57)   VOICE OF GOD

1.   Who heard the voice of God as "a still small voice"?
2.   Who heard the voice of God confirming his son ship.
3.   Which followers heard the voice of God?
4.   Who in the midst of persecuting God's people heard the voice of God?
5.   Who heard the voice of God out of the whirlwind?

(58)   DOUBT

1.   Who doubted God's power because of her age?
2.   Who because of fear did not believe that God would do what He said He would do?
3.   Who was the man that did not have confidence in himself and had to ask for signs?
4.   Who doubted when he was about doing a spectacular thing?
5.   Who in the face of persecution doubted the earlier prophecy he received?
6.   Who has been acclaimed globally as a super doubter

(59)   COURAGE

1.   Who agreed to offer his son to a covenant partner?
2.   Who preferred to be associated with slaves and suffered affliction than to remain in the palace where he was brought up?
3.   Which people had the courage to pass through walls of a big sea on dry land?
4.   Who singly pursued a host of the enemies and destroyed them with the exception of their leader?

5. Who was the son of an harlot that was thrown out of his father's house by the legal sons but later had the courage to go back and rule over his people?

6. Who after being defeated by the enemies gathered up courage to kill more people at his point of death than he killed in his life time

7. Who gathered up his courage when he was sent a second time to deliver a warning to a great city that was to be punished.

ANSWERS

1.) The Horses

1. c (Exod. 14:24-25)
2. e (I Kings 18:5)
3. g (Isa. 36:8)
4. f (2 Chron. 9:25)
5. I (2 Kings 14:17-20)
6. h (2 Kings 9:16-23)
7. b (I Chron. 18:3-5)
8. j (2 Kings 3:6-7)
9. d (I Kings 20:20)
10. a (Esther 6:7-11)

2.) ANGER

1. Saul (I Sam. 20:30-33)
2. Balak (Num. 24:10)
3. Jonah (Jonah 3:1-10; 4:1)
4. Moses (Exod. 32:4, 19-20)
5. Eliab (I Sam. 17:20, 28)
6. Haman (Esther 3:1-6)
7. Ahab (I Kings 21:1-4)
8. Naaman (2 Kings 5:9-12)
9. Nebuchadnezzar (Dan. 2:1-12)
10. Jacob (Gen. 31:26-37)
11. Moses (Numb,. 20: 1-13)
12. King Saul (1 Sam. 15)

3.) ANOINTING

1.   c (I Kings 19:16-20)
2.   e (Exod. 28:39-41) Read the whole of chapter 28
3.   g (Luke 7:37-38)
4.   f (2 Kings 9:1-6)
5.   i (Gen. 28:18)
6.   h (2 Chron. 23:11-15, 24:1)
7.   b (I Sam 9:17; 10:1)
8.   l (Dan. 10:2-3)
9.   d (I Sam. 16:1-13)
10.   a (I Kings 1:39-40)

4.) ARK OF GOD

1.   Ark is to be made according to God's instructions (Exod. 25:1; 10:22)
2.   Ark is used to divide the river Jordan (Josh. 3:14-17)
3.   Ark is carried in the march around Jericho's walls (Josh. 6:6-20)
4.   Philistines take the Ark (I Sam. 5:1)
5.   Philistines return the Ark (I Sam. 5:1)
6.   Ark remains at Kiriathjearim for 20 years (I Sam. 7:1-2)
7.   Uzzah touched the Ark and was killed (2 Sam. 6:6-8)
8.   Ark is brought to Obed-Edom's house (2 Sam. 6:10-11)
9.   Ark is brought to Jerusalem (2 Sam. 6:12-16)
10.   Ark is placed in Solomon's temple (I Kings 8:1-6)
11.   John sees the Ark in God's temple in heaven (Rev. 11:19)

5.) BATHING/WASHING

1.   Pharaoh's daughter (Exod. 2:5-6)
2.   Joseph (Gen. 43:29-31)
3.   Pilate (Matt. 27:24)
4.   Moses & Aaron (Exod. 40:30-32)
5.   Lot (Gen. 19:1-2)
6.   Jacob (Gen. 35:1-3)
7.   Laban (Gen. 24:29-32)

8.   David (2 Sam. 11:2)
9.   Job (Job 9:30)
10. Jesus (John 9:1, 7:11)

6.) COURAGEOUS PEOPLE

1.   f (Dan. 6:6-22)
2.   d (Num. 16:46-49)
3.   i (2 Sam. 23:11-12)
4.   h (Mark 15:43}
5.   j (I Sam. 17:4, 23-49)
6.   b (Judg. 7:7-22)
7.   e (Esther 4:11-16)
8.   c (2 Sam. 23:20)
9.   g (Neh. 6:10-11)
10. a (I Sam. 14:13-14)

7.) BUSINESS

1.   e. (Gen. 25:31-34)
2.   d (I Chron. 21:22-25)
3.   b (Acts 16:14)
4.   j (Neh. 13:15-19)
5.   g (Jer. 32:6-11)
6.   i (Acts 18:1-3)
7.   f (Gen. 23:10-18)
8.   c (2 Kings 4:2-7)
9.   a (Exod. 5:5-18)
10. h (Gen. 37:25-28)

8.) CHARIOTS

1.   David (2 Sam. 8:4)
2.   Zechariah (Zech. 6:1-3)
3.   Joseph (Gen. 41:42-43)

4.   Pharaoh (Exod. 14:23-28)
5.   Solomon (I Kings 10:26)
6.   Sisera (Judg. 4:1-3)
7.   Elisha (2 Kings 2:11-12)
8.   Jehu (2 Kings 9:16-20)
9.   Ahab (I Kings 22:34-38)
10.   Absalom (2 Sam. 15:1)

9.) CITIES

1.   j (I Kings 20:30-34)
2.   g (2 Chron. 32:1-3)
3.   h (I Kings 9:16-19)
4.   c (Judg. 1:11-16)
5.   i (Gen. 19:24-25)
6.   a (I Sam. 22:11, 17-19)
7.   e (Josh. 6:1-20)
8.   b (2 Kings 6:24-29)
9.   d (Acts 19:17-19)
10.   f (Judg. 9:45)

10.) CONFESSIONS

1.   Balaam (Num. 22:27-34)
2.   Achan (Josh. 7:18-25)
3.   Daniel (Dan. 9:3-5)
4.   Ezra (Ezra 10:1-2)
5.   Aaron (Lev. 16:21)
6.   John (John 1:19-20)
7.   Moses (Num. 21:6-7)
8.   Saul (I Sam. 15:24-27)
9.   Shimei (2 Sam. 16:5-6, 19:18-19)
10.   Pharaoh (Exod. 9:25-27)
11.   Woman with issue blood (Mk. 5:24-34)

11.) HIDING

1. Joshua (Josh. 10:16-18)
2. David (I Sam. 20:1, 5)
3. Joash (2Chron. 22:10-12)
4. Elijah (I Kings 17:2-6)
5. Obadiah (I Kings 18:4)
6. Rahab (Josh. 2:1-6)
7. Adam (Gen. 3:8)
8. Moses (Exod. 1:22; 2:2, 10)
9. Jesus (John 8:57-59)
10. Saul (I Sam. 10:21-22)

12.) JESUS

1. f (John 11:1-44)
2. g (John 2:1-11)
3. j (Matt. 3:13-16)
4. i (Mark 5:1-13)
5. a (Matt. 21:1-9)
6. c (Luke 4:14-17)
7. h (Matt. 26:36, 46-57)
8. d (Matt. 28:16-20)
9. e (Mark 1:21)
10. b (Luke 24:13-15)

13.) COVENANTS

1. Jacob (Gen. 31:43-48)
2. Jonathan (I Sam. 18:3-4)
3. Noah (Gen. 9:12-14)
4. Joshua (Josh. 24:25-27)
5. Isaac (Gen. 26:26-30)
6. Abraham (Gen. 17:2-5)
7. Nahash (I Sam. 11:1-2)

8. Benhadad (I Kings 20:33-34)
9. Moses (Deut. 5:1-5)
10. Jehoiada (2 Kings 11:17-18)
11. Jesus (Lk. 22:20)

14.) DEATH/MIRACLES

1. Jezebel (2 Kings 9:30-33)
2. Elisha (2 Kings 4:32-35)
3. Abimelech (Judges 9:53-54)
4. Dorcas (Acts 9:34-41)
5. Ahab (I Kings 22:34-37)
6. Aaron (Num. 20:28)
7. Lazarus (John 11:39-44)
8. Ananias (Acts 5:1-5)
9. Haman (Esther 7:9-10)
10. Ahithophel (2Sam. 17:23)

15.) DECEPTION

1. Rebekah (Gen. 27:15-20)
2. Jael (Judg. 4:17-21)
3. David (I Sam. 21:10-13)
4. Joshua (Josh. 9:3-16)
5. Jacob (Gen. 29:18-25)
6. Saul (I Sam. 28:8-12)
7. Abraham (Gen. 12:11-19) Isaac (Gen. 26:7-9)
8. Ehud (Judg. 3:18-22)
9. Joseph (Gen. 42:7-17)
10. Joab (2 Sam. 14:1-8)

16.) SWORDS

1. c (2 Sam. 23:9-10)
2. e (I Sam. 13:22)
3. g (Josh. 5:13)

4. f (Judg. 9:53-54)
5. i (John 18:10)
6. h (2 Sam. 2:12-16)
7. b (I Sam. 17:23-39)
8. j (2 Sam 20:9-10)
9. d (I Kings 3:16-27)
10. a (I Sam. 17:50-51)

17.) DREAM/VISIONS

1. j (Gen. 37:9)
2. e (Zech. 1:8)
3. d (Dan. 4:4-5, 10-11)
4. a (Isa. 6:1-8)
5. i (Gen. 28:1-16)
6. g (Dan. 7:1-5)
7. b (Judge 7:13)
8. c (Acts 10:10-16)
9. f (Gen. 41:17-24)
10. h (Gen. 31:22-24)
11. k (Acts 7:55-59)

18.) ESCAPES

1. j (Acts 9:23-25)
2. h (I Sam. 22:18-20)
3. g (Gen. 27:42-43)
4. i (I Kings 19:1-3)
5. c (Gen. 19:17-22)
6. e (Matt. 2:13-14)
7. a (I Kings 20:19-20)
8. d (I Sam. 19:10-18)
9. b (Judges 3:21-27)
10. f (John 11:53-57)

19.) ALTAR MATTERS

1. Abraham (Gen. 22:1, 2, 6-13)
2. Paul (Acts 17:16, 23)
3. Gideon (Judg. 6:25-32)
4. Ahaz (2 Kings 16:10)
5. Joshua (Josh. 8:30-32)
6. Uzziah (2 Chron. 26:16-21)
7. Joab (I Kings 2-5, 29-34)
8. Jeroboam (I Kings 13:1-4)
9. Isaac (Gen. 26:23-25)
10. Josiah (2 Kings 23:16)

20.) SPY

1. Moses (Num. 13:17-25)
2. Rahab (Josh. 2:1-6)
3. Hanun (2 Sam. 10:2-4)
4. Jesus (Luke 20:20-26)
5. Joseph (Gen. 42:6-9)
6. Caleb (Josh. 14:7-9, 14)
7. Micah (Judg. 18:13-18)
8. Paul (Gal. 2:4)
9. Absalom (2 Sam. 15:10)
10. David (I Sam. 26:3, 4)

21.) FAMILY AFFAIRS

1. Jehoshabeath (2 Chron. 22:10-11)
2. Abimelech (Judg. 9:4-5)
3. Lois (2 Tim. 1:5)
4. Jethro (Exod. 18:14-24)
5. Hagar (Gen. 21:14-16)
6. Miriam (Exod. 2:3-8)
7. Jonathan (1 Sam. 20:32-34)

8.   Abraham (Gen. 14:12-16)
9.   Jesse (1 Sam. 16:8-12)
10. Jezebel (1 Kings 21:4-8)
11. Job's wife (Job 2:9)
12. Paul's Nephew (Acts 23:16-22)
13. Virgin Mary (Lk 1:39-41)
14. Jesus (Lk 8:19-21)
15. Jacob (Gen. 29:10-14
16. Sennacherib, King of Assyria (2 Kings 19:35-37)

22.) FARM MATTERS

1.   Boaz (Ruth 3:1-4)
2.   Jesus (Luke 6:1)
3.   Gideon (Judg. 6:11)
4.   Uzziah (2 Chron. 26:10-11)
5.   Joab (2 Sam 14:28-32)
6.   Job (Job 1:14-15)
7.   Isaac (Gen 26:12)
8.   Joseph (Gen 47:13-25)
9.   Samson (Judg. 15:4-5)
10. Naboth (1 Kings 21:1-3; 9-10)

23.) FASTING

1.   g (2 Sam 12:15, 16)
2.   d (Acts 9:8-9)
3.   h (Matt. 4:1, 3)
4.   j (1 Kings 21:20, 27)
5.   i (Esther 4:15-16)
6.   c (Exod. 34:2, 28)
7.   a (Neh. 1:2-4)
8.   b (Acts 10:30)
9.   f (Dan. 6:16-18)
10. e (1 Kings 19:5-8)

24.) FEAR

1.   Eliphaz (Job 4:1, 13-15)
2.   Jacob (Gen. 32:3-7)
3.   Saul (1 Sam 28:4-5)
4.   Manoah (Judg. 13:20-22)
5.   Belshazzar (Dan. 5:5-6)
6.   Jonah (Jonah 1:3-15)
7.   Aaron & Israelites (Exod. 34:29-30)
8.   Peter (Matt. 14:29-30)
9.   Israelites (Exod. 14:7-10)
10. Peter, James, John (Matt. 17:1, 5-7)

25.) CELEBRATIONS

1.   Belshazzar (Dan. 5:1-5)
2.   Job (Job 1:1, 4-5)
3.   Nabal (1 Sam. 25:36-37)
4.   Abraham (Gen. 21:8)
5.   Ahasuerus (Esther 1:2-5, 9)
6.   Samson (Judg. 14:10-13)
7.   Pharaoh (Gen 40:20)
8.   Levi (Luke 5:27-29)
9.   Abner (2 Sam. 3:19-20)
10. Solomon (1 Kings 8:64, 65)
11. The Prodigal son (Luke 15:11-32)

26.) GATES

1.   f (2 Sam. 15:2-6)
2.   j (Acts 12:7-10)
3.   k (2 Kings 7:1)
4.   a (Acts 12:13-14)
5.   i (2 Sam. 18:4)
6.   h (Neh. 8:1-3)
7.   g (Judges 16:3)
8.   e (Jer. 39:4)

9.   b (2 Sam. 3:27-30)
10. d (Ruth 4:1-9)
11. c (Jer. 20:1-2)

27.) GIFTS

1.   Jacob (Gen. 32:11-20)
2.   Hezekiah (2 Kings 20:12-13)
3.   Daniel (Dan. 2:45-48)
4.   Rebekah (Gen. 24:10-22)
5.   Benhadad (2 Kings 8:7-9)
6.   Saul (I Sam. 9:7-8)
7.   Job (Job 42:10-11)
8.   Jesus (Matt. 2:7-11)
9.   Hiram (I Kings 9:11)
10. Queen of Sheba (2 Chron. 9:1-9)

28.) JEALOUSY

1.   Saul (I Sam. 18:6-9)
2.   Cain (Gen. 4:3-8)
3.   Joshua (Num. 11:26-29)
4.   Jesus (Matt. 27:1-2, 11-18)
5.   Isaac (Gen. 26:12-16)
6.   Prodigal Son (Luke 15:11-30)
7.   Sarah (Gen. 21:9-14)
8.   Joseph (Gen. 37:4-28)
9.   Paul and Barnabas (Acts 13:43-50)
10. Rachel (Gen. 29:31; 30:1)

29.) HAIR

1.   Hannah (I Sam. 1:11)
2.   Ezekiel (Ezek. 8:3)
3.   Absalom (2 Sam. 14:25-26)
4.   Eliphaz (Job 4:13-15)

5. Paul (I Tim. 2:9)
6. Samson (Jud. 16:17-19)
7. Elisha (2 Kings 2:23, 24)
8. Nebuchadnezzar (Dan. 4:33)
9. Jesus (Luke 12:6-7)
10. Esau (Gen. 27:1-35)

30.) HEAVEN

1. Moses (Exod. 16:3-4)
2. Nebuchadnezzar (Dan. 4:10-13)
3. Abram (Gen. 15:5)
4. Solomon (2 Chron. 7:1)
5. Peter (Acts 10:11)
6. Jesus (Matt. 3:16)
7. Joshua (Josh. 10:12-13)
8. Elijah (2 Kings 2:11)
9. Ezekiel (Ezek. 1:1)
10. David (I Chron. 21:16)
11. Descendants of Noah (Gen. 11:1-8)
12. Stephen (Acts 7:56)

31.) EARTHQUAKE

1. Moses (Exod. 19:17-18)
2. Jonathan (I Sam. 14:14-15)
3. Elijah (I Kings 19:11)
4. John (Rev. 11:13)
5. Jesus (Matt. 27:50-51)
6. Paul and Silas (Acts 16:25-26)
7. Koran, Dathan, Abiram (Num. 16:1, 3, 31-32)
8. Mary and Mary Magdalene (Matt. 28:1-2)
9. David (2 Sam. 2:1, 8)
10. Uzziah (Zech. 14:5, Amos 1:1)

32.) ELIJAH OR ELISHA?

1. Elisha (2Kings 4:38-41)
2. Both (2 Kings 2:8-14)
3. Elisha (2 Kings 4:42-44)
4. Both (I Kings 17:17-24; 2 Kings 4:20, 32-35)
5. Elijah (I Kings 18:36-38)
6. Elisha (2 Kings 5:1-14)
7. Both (I Kings 17:10-16; 2 Kings 4:2-6)
8. Elisha (2 Kings 2:19-22)
9. Elisha (2 Kings 6:5-6)
10. Elijah (2 Kings 1:9-12)
11. Elisha (2 Kings 6:11-24)
12. Elisha (2 Kings 2:23-24)
13. Elisha (2 Kings 8:11-12)
14. Elijah (I Kings 17:1)
15. Elisha (2 Kings 5:17-27)
16. Elisha (1 Kings 19:19-20)
17. Elisha (2 Kings 13:20-21)
18. Elisha (2 Kings 4:8-17)
19. Elijah (2 Kings 2:11-12)

33.) MARTYRS

1. Bartholomew
2. Mark
3. James the less
4. Phillip
5. John
6. Andrew
7. Simon (Zelotes)
8. Matthew
9. Peter
10. Luke
11. Stephen
12. John the Baptist
13. Mathias

14. Paul
15. James the Great
16. Thomas
17. Jude

34.) ANGELS

1.   l On Mount Olive (Lk. 22:43)
2.   d Under an Oak tree (Judges 6:11-21
3.   i Prison (Acts 12:7)
4.   k Tent door (Gen. 18:1-2)
5.   h Field (Lk. 2:8-9)
6.   g Threshing Floor (I Chron. 21:15-25)
7.   j Wilderness Spring (Gen. 16:6-11)
8.   f Under a Juniper tree (I Kgs. 19:5-8)
9.   b House (Acts 10:30-33)
10. c City Gate (Gen. 19:1ff)
11. e Sepulcher (John 20:11-14)
12. a As she sat in the field (Judges 13:3-21)

35.) KINGS

1.   Jeroboam (I Kgs. 14:1-18)
2.   Rehoboam, Son of Solomon (I Kgs. 14:31)
3.   Ahab, husband of Jezebel (II Kgs. 10:1-11)
4.   Joash; the Prophet was Elisha (II Kgs. 13:14-19)
5.   Ahaz (II Kgs. 16:1-4)
6.   Hezekiah (II Kgs. 18:13-19:37)
7.   Manaseh (II Kgs. 21:1)
8.   Jeroboam (I Kgs. 13:1-6)
9.   King Agryppa (Herod) (Acts 12:1-23)
10. Herod Phillip (Mark 6:17, Matt. 14:3)
11. Saul (I Sam. 10:9-13; 28:7-8)
12. King Belshazzar (Dan. 5:1-2)
13. Ahab (I Kgs. 21:14-26)

36.) GOD'S MESSENGERS

1. Moses (Ex. 3-4)
2. Samuel (I Sam. 3)
3. Esther (Esther 5, 6, 7)
4. King Ahasuerus (Esther 8:10-9:25)
5. Mordecai (Esther 2:1-20)
6. Joseph (Gen. 41)
7. John the Baptist (Lk. 1:13-17; John 1)
8. Peter (Acts 10)
9. Jesus—This means "Salvation from Yahweh.
    The story of Hi s saving the lost is presented by the Gospels.
10. Joshua (Joshua 1:2-9) All his deeds are in the book of Joshua.

37.) GOD'S INTERVENTION

1. h (Ex. 14:8-31)
2. g (Ex. 13:21-22)
3. e (Ex. 12:1-32)
4. c (Dan. 6:7-24)
5. b (Dan. 3:1-27)
6. d (I Sam. 17:1-57)
7. a (2 Kings 6:8-22)
8. f (Prov. 11:5)
9. i (Esther 5:14-6:10)

38.) THOSE WHO HAD THEIR NAMES CHANGED

The following are the new names

1. Israel—God gave him a new name (Gen. 35:10)
2. Joshua or Jehoshua—Moses changed his name—(Num. 13:8, 16)
3. Peter—Jesus gave him this name (Matt. 16:18)
4. Paul—The change of name was after his conversion.
    / He was first called Paul in (Acts 13:9)

5.   Belteshazzar—The prince of the Eunuchs (Ashpenaz) in Babylon gave him this name when the Israelites were taken captives (Dan. 1:7)

6.   Shedrack—This was his Babylonian name given by the Chief of Eunuchs (Dan. 1:7)

7.   Meshack—His Babylonian name given by the Chief of Eunuchs (Dan.1:7)

8.   Abednego—This was his Babylonian name given by the Chief of Eunuchs (Dan. 1:7)

9.   Benjamin—Given by his father (Gen. 35:18)

10. Abraham—Given by God (Gen. 17:5)

11. Sarah—Given by God (Gen. 17:15)

12. Esther—Given by her senior cousin, Mordecai (Esther 2:7)

39.) BIBLE COMMON NAMES

(1) JUDAS

a.   The brother of the Lord Jesus. (Matt. 13:55)

b.   Judas of Galilee was one of those who led a revolt against the Romans and died as a result.

c.   Paul after his encounter with God went to the house of Judas who lived in Straight Street. (Act 9:7-12)

d.   Judas surnamed Barsabbas chosen with Paul and Barnabas to deliver the letter from James to the Church in Antioch. (Acts 15:22)

e.   Judas a disciple of Jesus—usually called the brother of James (Lk. 6:16, Acts 1:13). His recorded word was found in John 14:22

f.   Judas Iscariot a disciple of Jesus who betrayed Him (Lk. 6:16, Matt. 26:20-21, Jn. 6:71)

(2) ELIEZER

a.   Servant of Abram who would have been his heir if Abraham did not have an heir Gen. 15:2

b.   Second son of Moses and Zipporah—Ex. 18:4

c.   One of the sons of Becher the son of Benjamin—I Chron. 7:6-8

d.   One of the priests who blew the trumpets when the ark of the covenant was brought to Jerusalem I Chron. 15:24

e.   A ruler of the Reubenites I Chron. 27:16

f.   Son of Dadavah who prophesied against Jehoshaphat 2 Chron. 20:37

g.   One of the leaders whom Ezra sent for Ezra 8:16
h.   A Levite who put away his foreign wife—Ezra 10:23
i.   A priest who put away his foreign wife with—Ezra 10:18

(3) MARY
a.   Mary the mother of Jesus—Lk 2:2-38
b.   Mary Magdalene—One of the women who followed and supported Jesus—Mark 15:40
c.   Mary of Bethany—sister of Martha and Lazarus—Lk 10:38-42, 11:11-14
d.   Mary mother of James, the younger and Joses—She was an eye witness at the death, burial and resurrection of Jesus—Matt 27:56-28:1, Mk 15:40, 16:1, Lk 24:10
e.   Mary the wife of Cleopas, the sister of Mary the mother of Jesus—Jn 19:25
f.   Mary the mother of John Mark. Peter went to her house after the prison release. It was a regular house for believers' meetings—Acts 12:12
g.   Mary from Rome. A Roman—Rom 16:6. A believer in Rome greeted by Paul who noted her care on the apostles' behalf in the Epistle of Romans.

(4) TAMAR
a.   Daughter-in-law of Judah, wife of his eldest son, Er.—Gen 38:6-11ff
b.   Daughter of David, raped by her half-brother Amnon—2 Sam 13.
c.   Absalom's only daughter was named Tamar—2 Sam 14:27
d.   Fortified city at the south of the Dead sea marking the ideal limit of Israel—Eze 47:19; 48:28

(5) SIMON
a.   Father of Judas Iscariot—John 6:71
b.   Simon Peter, Jesus disciple; a son of Jonah & the brother of Andrew—Matt 16:16-17
c.   The Pharisee who hosted Jesus at a dinner called Simon the leper—Lk. 7:36-50, Matt 26:6-13, Mk. 14:3
d.   Native of Cyrene forced to carry Jesus' cross—Mk 15:21
e.   Tanner of animal skin who lived in Joppa where Peter stayed—Acts 9:43
f.   Jesus' disciple called the Canaanite—Matt 10:4
g.   Brother of Jesus—Matt 13:55
h.   Magician from Samaria who believed Philip's preaching, got baptized and then try to buy the power of laying of hands—Acts 8:9-24

(6) JOSEPH
a.   Husband of Mary, the mother of Jesus—Matt 1:16, Jn. 1:45, Lk 2:4
b.   Joseph of Arimathea who collected the body of Jesus and laid him in his own tomb—Mark 15:45-46
c.   A brother of Jesus named after his father called Joses—Matt 13:55
d.   Another name for Barsabas who was not elected when a replacement was chosen for Judas—Acts 1:23

(7) JOEL
a.   Son of Samuel who became an evil judge causing the introduction of kingship in Israel—I Sam 8:2
b.   A Levite—a descendent of Levi—I Chron 6:36
c.   A member of tribe of Reuben—I Chron 5:4, 8
d.   Leader among the Levites under David who brought the Ark to Jerusalem—I Chron 23:8, 26:22
e.   Member of tribe of Simeon—I Chron 4:35
f.   Leader of the tribe of Gad—I Chron 5:12
g.   Leader of the tribe of Issachar—I Chron 7:3
h.   Military hero under David—I Chron 11:38
i.   Leader of Western half of the tribe of Manasseh under David—I Chron 27:20
j.   Levite who helped King Hezekiah cleanse the temple—2 Chron 29:12
k.   Israelite condemned by Ezra for having a foreign wife who might lead the nation to worship other gods—Ezra 10:43
l.   Leader of the people from the tribe of Benjamin living in Jerusalem at the time of Nehemiah—Neh. 11:9
m.   Prophet Joel who wrote the Book of Joel. He was the son of Pethuel—Joel 1:1

(8) DEBORAH
a.   Rebecca's nurse—Gen 35:8
b.   A judge in Israel, a prophetess and wife of Lapidoth—Judge 4:4-5

(9) SIMEON
a.   One of the 12 sons of Jacob, the second Son of Leah—Gen 29:33 and ancestor of Jesus—Lk 3:30
b.   Devout Jew who lived in Jerusalem during the time of Jesus birth—Lk 2:25
c.   Prophet and teacher in the church at Antioch called Niger—Acts 13:1

(10) JAMES
a.   Son of Zebedee and brother of John—Matt. 10:2; Mk. 1:19; 3:17, Lk 5:10
b.   The son of Alphaeus, a disciple—Matt. 10:3; Mk. 3:18; Lk. 6:15; Acts 1:13
c.   The brother of Jesus—Matt. 13:55; Mk. 6:3

(11) JONATHAN
a.   Levite who served as a priest of Micah in Ephraim—Judges 17:8
b.   Eldest son of King Saul, the friend of David—I Sam. 18:1-4; 19:1-7; 20:1-42; 23:16-18
c.   Son of Abiathar the priest in service to David—I Kg. 1:42-43
d.   An uncle of David who worked as counselor and scribe in the royal court—I Chron. 27:32
e.   Son of Shimei, David's brother who slew a Philistine giant—2 Sam. 21:21; I Chron. 20:6-7
f.   Son of Shammah; one of David's 37 mighty men—2 Sam. 23:32-33; I Chron. 11:34
g.   Son of Uzziah—a royal treasurer in David's reign I Chron. 27:25
h.   Father of Ebed, a returned exile—Ezra 8:6
i.   Priest under Joiakim the high priest—Neh. 12:14
j.   Priest, son of Joiada—Neh. 12:11
k.   Priest, son of Shemaiah and father of Zechariah in a group who played musical instruments Neh. 12:35
l.   Son of Asahel who supported foreign marriages in the time of Ezra—Ezra 10:15
m.   Son of Jada, the son of Jerahmeel—I Chron. 2:32-33

(12) JOSHUA
a.   Leader of the Israelites who first took control of the Promised land of Canaan. The successor of Moses, the son of Nun—Joshua 1:1
b.   The high priest of the community who returned from Babylonian exile—Zechariah 3:1-5

(13) JUDAH
a.   The fourth son of Jacob. He was the ancestor of the tribe of Judah. The mother was Leah. The father in law of Tamar who had Pharez and Zarah (twins) for him Gen. 38

b.   Judah, the name of the southern kingdom inherited by the son of Solomon, Rehoboam, when the kingdom was divided after Solomon's death—I Kgs. 12:19-24

c.   Priest whose sons helped Zerubbabel and Joshua, the high priest on the work of restoring the temple after the exile—Ezra 3:9, Neh. 12:8

d.   Levite whom Ezra condemned for having foreign wife who might tempt Israel to worship other gods—Ezra 10:23

e.   Member of the tribe of Benjamin who lived in Jerusalem after the exile—Neh. 11:9, 12:34, 36. He also helped in Nehemiah's celebrations.

f.   The name of a city "City of Judah" 2Chron. 25:28, The city is Jerusalem.

(14) GAIUS

a.   Macedonian Christian who was one of Paul's traveling companions—Acts 19:29ff

b.   Christian from Derbe who accompanied Paul into Asia Acts 20:4

c.   Apostle Paul's host in Corinth—Rom. 16:23

d.   The Christian John loved and to whom he addressed (3 John 1)

(15) ELIHU

a.   Son of Barachel the Buzite who addressed Job after Job's three friends had ended their speeches—Job 32:2

b.   Samuel's great grand father—I Sam. 1:1

c.   Member of the tribe of Manasseh who deflected to David—I Chron. 12:20-21

d.   Mighty military hero under David—I Chron. 26:7-8

e.   One of David's brethren in charge of the tribe of Judah—I Chron. 27:18

40.) INJURIES

1.   Ahaziah (2 Kings 1:2)
2.   Jacob (Gen. 32:24, 25)
3.   Balaam (Num. 22:25)
4.   Abimelech (Judg. 9: 53-54)
5.   Solomon (I Kings 3:16-28)
6.   Mephibosheth (2 Sam. 4:4)

7.   Job (Job 1:2; 18-19)
8.   Absalom (2 Sam. 18:9)
9.   Eli (I Sam. 4:13, 18)
10. Paul (Acts 28:3)

41.) SIGNS AND WONDERS

1.   Upon Egypt, upon Pharaoh and upon all his household—Deut. 6:22, Ex. 7:8-10
2.   The Israelites Deut. 7:19
3.   Moses—Deut. 13:1-5
4.   The curses in Deuteronomy 28:14-46 (28:45-46)
5.   I and the children the Lord had given me—Is. 8:8
6.   Jesus—Matt. 24:23-24, Mk. 13:22
7.   The Galileans—John 4:45-48
8.   The Apostles—Acts 2:43
9.   Paul and Barnabas—Acts 15:12
10. God—Job 9:10 (NIV)

42.) CONSPIRACIES

1.   Rezin the king of Syria and Pekah the king of Israel—Israel 7:1-16
2.   Absalom—2 Sam. 15:1-18
3.   Zimri—I Kgs 16:8-10
4.   Joseph—Gen. 37:2-28
5.   Ahimelech—I Sam. 22:11-19
6.   Paul—Acts 23:11-15
7.   Samson—Judges 16:4-21
8.   Joash—2Kgs 12:19-20
9.   Daniel—Dan. 6:3-17
10. Sanballat and Tobiah—Neh. 4:7-8
11. Jesus—Matt. 26:3, 4:14-16
12. Ananias and Sapphira his wife—Acts 5:1-10
13. Jacob and Rebekah his mother—Gen. 27:1-23
14. King Jeroboam and wife—I Kgs 14:1-18

43.) MOTHERS

1. Rachel, Joseph's mother—Gen. 31:19-35
2. Mother of Ichabod, the wife of Phinehas—I Sam. 4:19-22
3. Naomi, mother of Mahlon and Chilion—Ruth 1:1-5
4. Eunice, mother of Timothy—2 Tim. 1:5, 3:15
5. Hannah, mother of Samuel—I Sam. 1:5-18
6. Mother of Zebedee brothers, (John and James) Matt. 20:20-23
7. Mary, the mother of Jesus—Lk. 2:42-48
8. Elizabeth, mother of John the Baptist Lk. 1:57-64, Matt. 3:4
9. King Lamuel's mother Prov. 31:1-9
10. Meshullemeth, King Amon's mother—II Kgs 21:18-24
11. Maacha, the mother of King Asa—II Chron. 15:16-19; IKgs. 15:8-13
12. King Belshazzar's mother—the queen—Dan. 5:1-12
13. Jochebed Moses' mother—Ex. 2:1-4, 6:20
14. Keturah—Gen. 25:1-2
15. Sarah, mother of Isaac—Gen. 17:17; 21:5
16. Leah, the mother of Simeon, Levi, Reuben etc. the senior sister of Rachel—Gen. 29:31-35; 30:16-21
17. Hagar, mother of Ishmael—Gen. 21:9-20
18. Gomer, the wife of Prophet Hosea—Hosea 1:3-9
19. Sarah, mother of Isaac Gen. 24:67
20. Abigail, mother of Amasa—I Chron. 2:16-17
21. Zipporah, the wife of Moses—Ex. 4:25

44.) FATHERS

1. Jesse—I Sam. 16:1-13
2. David—2 Sam. 15:1-13
3. King Saul—I Sam. 20:27-34
4. Eli—I Sam. 2:22-23
5. Jonathan—2 Sam. 9:1-13
6. Abraham—Gen. 24:1-4
7. Isaac—Gen. 27:1-23ff
8. Laban—Gen. 29:14-30
9. Manoah—Judges 13

10. Jacob—Gen. 29:31-30:17-18, 34:1
11. Zacharias—Lk. 1:5, 62-64
12. Judah—Gen. 38:6-11
13. Bethuel—Gen. 22:23; 24:15-67
14. Abihail—Esther 2:15

45.) SERVANTS

1. Elisha—2kgs. 2: 12-14
2. Gehazi servant of Elisha—2Kgs. 4:25-27
3. Samuel—I Sam. 3:1, 11:18
4. Ziba—2 Sam 9:1-13
5. Eliezer, Abraham's servant—Gen. 15:2
6. Onesimus—Philemon vs 10-16
7. Hagar—Gen. 16:1-16
8. Zilpah—Maid-servant of Leah mother of Asher and Gad Gen. 30:10-13
9. Bilhah-maid servant of Rachel—Gen. 30:3-6
10. Abraham eldest servant—Gen. 24:1-9ff
11. Moses—Num. 20:1-12, Joshua 1:12-13
12. Joseph—Gen. 39

46.) ACTIONS

1. k (Mark 5:24-34)
2. d (2Kings 5:1, 9-14)
3. h (Judg. 16:1-3)
4. j (Gen. 32:24)
5. i (Exod. 15:20-21)
6. c (2Sam. 18:18-23)
7. a (Lk. 19:1-9)
8. b (2Sam. 22:29-31)
9. f (IKgs 18:42-46)
10. e (Matt. 14:25-29)
11. g (2kgs. 9: 11-20)

47.) BUILDINGS

1. Nehemiah—Neh. 4: 6-17
2. Israelites _Ex.5: 6-14
3. Solomon—1 kgs.6:1-7
4. Noah—Gen.6:13-16
5. Bezaleel—Ex. 35: 30-35
6. Jotham—2 Chron. 27:1-4
7. Hiram—1 kgs. 7:13-45
8. David—1 Chron. 22:2-8
9. Joshua—Josh.6:26
10. Cain—Gen. 4:17
11. Tower of Babel—Gen. 11: 3-9

48.) PRAISES AND SONGS

1. c (Rev. 14:3)
2. e (2 Chron. 35:25)
3. g (2 Chron. 20:18-22)
4. f (Deut. 31:30; 32:1-44)
5. i (I Sam. 18:6-8)
6. h (Judg. 4:10, 5:1-31)
7. b (Acts 16:25)
8. j (Num. 21:17-18ff)
9. d (2 Sam. 1:17-27)
10. a (Mark 14:26)
11. Miriam (Ex. 15:20-21)
12. Joshua and the Israelites at the fall of Jericho walls (Josh. 6:6-25)
13. Hannah (I Sam. 2:1-10)
14. Virgin Mary (Lk. 1:46-55)
15. Zacharias (Lk. 1:67-79)
16. Simeon who was waiting for the consolation of Israel (Lk. 2:5-32)
17. Paul and Silas (Acts 16:19-28)
18. Nebuchadnezzar, King of Babylon (Dan. 4:34-37)

49.) HOSPITALITY

1. Abraham Gen 18
2. The Shunammite woman. 2 kgs 4; 8-10
3. Manoah—Judges 13 : 15-16 (Read ch. 13)
4. Lot—Gen 19.
5. Zacchaeus—Lk 19: 1-10
6. Lydia—Acts 16:14-15
7. Samuel—I Sam 9:22-24
8. Moses—EX. 2:15-22
9. Jesus—Lk 5:27-32
10. Laban—Gen 24:24-33

50.) LETTERS

1. David to Joab on Uriah—2 Sam 11:13-24
2. Jezebel—1 kgs 21: 1-15
3. Elijah to Jehoram—2 Chro.21:1-15
4. King of Syria to king of Israel on Naaman—2 kgs 5
5. Hezekiah—2 Chro. 30:1-13
6. Sennacherib to Hezekiah Is. 37:9-14.
7. Artaxerxes Exra 4.
8. The Apostles—Acts 15:22-29
9. Jehu—2 kgs 10:1-8.
10. Claudius Lysias to Felix—Acts 23:16-30

51.) DRUNKENNESS

1. Noah—Gen 9:20-21
2. Nabal—1 Sam 25: 36-37
3. Belshazzar—Dan 5:1-5
4. Lot—Gen. 19:31-36
5. Elah—1 kings 16:8-10
6. Corinthians Church—1 Cor 11:20-22
7. Benhadad king of Syria—1 kings 20:1-20.

52.) DISOBEDIENCE

1.   Adam and Eve—Gen 3
2.   Achan—Josh.7
3.   Pharoah—Ex.5:1-10
4.   Jonah—Jonah 1.
5.   Saul—1 Sam 15.
6.   Man of God from Judah—1 kings 13:1-29
7.   Moses—Num. 20: 1-13

53.) MURDER

1.   Cain—Gen 4:1-10
2.   Abimelech—Judges 9:1-6
3.   Joab—2 Sam 3:12, 12-30
4.   David—2 Sam 11, 12:1-10
5.   Jezebel—1 kings 21
6.   Shallum—2 kings 15:8-11
7.   Amon—2 kings 21:18-24
8.   John the Baptist—Mark 6:16-28
9.   Sennacherib—2 kgs 19:36-37

54.) FAITHFULNESS

1.   Abraham—Gen. 22
2.   Daniel—Dan 6:3-22
3.   Paul—Acts 20:17-24
4.   Moses—Num 12:1-8
5.   Joseph—Gen 39:1-20
6.   Timothy—1 Cor.4:17
7.   David—1 Sam 22:9-16
8.   Jonathan—1 Sam 20:1-42,23:16-18

55.) PRAYERS

1. Paul and Silas—Acts 16:16-28
2. Jabez—1 Chro. 4:9-10
3. Joshua—Josh 7:2-12
4. Abraham—Gen. 18:23-33
5. Hannah—1 Sam.1: 9-17
6. Elijah—1 kings.18:36-39
7. Hezekiah—II kings. 20:1-6
8. Daniel—Dan 9:2-22
9. Jonah—Jonah 2
10. Peter—Acts 9:36-41
11. Anna—Lk 2:36-38
12. Jesus—John 11:14-45
13. Jehoshaphat—2 Chro 20:1-13

56.) PROPHETS

1. Aaron—Ex 7:1-2
2. Balaam—Numb. 24.
3. Elijah—I Kgs 18
4. Elisha—2 Kgs 6:8-20
5. Ezekiel—Ezek. 1.
6. Deborah—Judges 4:1-15
7. Hosea—Hosea 1
8. Amos—7:10-17
9. Isaiah—2 kgs 20:1-11
10. Nathan—2 Sam 11-12.

57.) VOICE OF GOD

1. Elijah—I kgs 19:9-17
2. Jesus Christ at baptism—Matt 3:16-17.
3. Peter, James and John at transfiguration—Matt 17: 3-8
4. Paul—Acts 9:1-9
5. Job—Job 40

58.) DOUBT

1. Sarah—Gen 18:1-15
2. Moses—Ex 4:1-17
3. Gideon—Judges 6;
4. Peter—Matt. 14:22-33
5. John the Baptist—Lk 7:18-23
6. Thomas—John 20:24-31

59.) COURAGE

1. Abraham
2. Moses
3. Israelites
4. Barak—Judges 4 : 12-16
5. Jephthah—Judges 11 :1-11
6. Samson—Judges 16 : 23-30
7. Jonah—Jonah 3: 1-5

REFERENCES

i   Holman Illustrated Bible Dictionary

ii   Do you know your Bible? By Erma Reynolds.

www.ingramcontent.com/pod-product-compliance
Lightning Source LLC
Chambersburg PA
CBHW021232280526
45784CB00005B/2065